FSC
www.fsc.org

MIX

Papier aus ver-
antwortungsvollen
Quellen
Paper from
responsible sources

FSC® C105338

Izabela Luiza Jahn

Wisdom

Imprint

Bibliographic information of the German National Library:
The German National Library lists this publication in the German
National Bibliography; detailed bibliographic data are available on the
Internet at http://dnb.dnb.de.

© 2023 Izabela Luiza Jahn

Cover photo: Izabela Luiza Jahn

Production and publisher: BoD - Books on Demand, Norderstedt

ISBN: 978-3-7583-1121-5

"Wisdom comes with age. To some people, however, age comes alone." - Miłosz Brzeziński

F O R E W O R D

Wisdom does not fall from the sky. It does not come through the passage of time. Expertise is necessary to get through life, but wisdom is more:

"Wisdom" (Old Greek σοφία, Latin sapientia, Hebrew hokhmah) refers primarily to a profound understanding of interrelationships in nature, life, and society, as well as the ability to identify the most coherent and sensible course of action in the face of problems and challenges.

There are several definitions and concepts of wisdom, which usually move in the spaces of tension between rationality and intuition, knowledge and faith, and experience and instinct. There is broad agreement on the view that wisdom is evidence of mental agility and independence: it enables its bearer to systematically do things

- to think ("a wise insight," "a wise decision," "a wise judgment"),
- to say ("a wise word", "a wise counsel") or
- to do ("a wise behavior"),

that prove to be sustainably meaningful in the given situation. This often happens while avoiding disturbing influences, such as one's own emotional state or social peer pressure. However, on closer examination and comprehensive appreciation of all circumstances, sometimes only with temporal or spatial distance, these considerations, statements and actions prove to be "correct", applicable or "true". The same applies to words and actions that the wise man does not utter or do after careful consideration (cf. "Si tacuisses, philosophus mansisses"). Wisdom is counted among the cardinal virtues." [1]

Mine just tells me I should rather drop the subject, because what do I know. Spoken with Socrates: "I know that I do not know". And that's why this will be a collection of wise stories, which are certainly not mine.

Followed by things I painfully learned thanks to my own stupidity. Read for yourself.

THE
STORIES

There is only one sign of wisdom: good humor that lasts.
- Michel de Montaigne

According to the aforementioned definition, in that case we are certainly not dealing with a "blissful idiot" who understands nothing but has little sorrow as a result. A wise person understands and knows that life is difficult and has its burdens and inevitably brings pain. But he also knows that, as Buddha said, pain is inevitable, but suffering is optional. If I don't let go of the pain and wrestle with it and feel it as a great injustice, pulling my hair out and complaining "why me?", then I create the suffering.

It is therefore a question of the inner mental attitude to things. Also to the ability to see the light in the shadows, i.e.to be able, even in "bad times", to perceive and acknowledge the nevertheless inevitably beautiful moments therein. To take pleasure in "little things": in nature, in a friendly gesture, in being alive, in the fact that the water comes from the tap, that we lead a privileged life in continental Europe.

Not taking things for granted or as a birthright proves to be very helpful to look at them with gratitude. When you realize what a great gift all this is, how could you still be in a bad mood?

I'm afraid I don't remember who said it, but the gist was: "If you see His Holiness the Dalai Lama for 60 seconds, you've seen him laugh at least three times..."

"But how can I laugh when everything around me is bad, when there is nothing good that even gets through to me that I let get to me, when the heart is heavy and life is just black wasteland?"

If this is, how you feel, so the following story of the king's ring comes to my mind:

"A king once consulted the wise men in his court and said to them, "I am having a beautiful ring made. I have the best diamonds that can be obtained. I want to have a hidden message in the ring that can help me in times of utter despair. It must be very short so that it can be hidden under the diamond of the ring." All the sages, all the great scholars could have written long treatises on this. But to give him a message that contained only two or three words and would help him in times of greatest despair... They thought, they looked in their books, but they could find nothing. The king had an old servant who was almost like a father to him. He had already been his father's servant. The king's mother had died early, and this servant had taken care of him. Therefore, he was not treated like a servant, and the king had great respect for him. The old man said, "I am not a wise man, I am not educated and I am not learned, but I know the message. For there is only one message. These men cannot give it to you. Only a mystic, someone who has known himself, can give it to you. During my long life in the palace, I have met all kinds of people, including once a mystic. He was a guest of your father, and I was assigned to him as a servant. When he left, as a gesture of thanks for my services, he gave me this message..." And he wrote it on a small slip of paper, folded it up, and said to the king, "Do not read it now. Keep it hidden in your ring and open it only when all has failed, when there is no way out." That time was soon to come. The country was invaded and the king lost his kingdom. He had to flee on his horse to save his life, and the enemy horsemen pursued him. He was alone; they outnumbered him. He came to a place where he had to stop because the road was over - he was standing on a cliff above a deep precipice. Falling down there would have been the end. He couldn't go back because the enemies were there, and he could already hear the hooves of their horses. He could not go forward, and there was no other way. Suddenly he remembered the ring. He opened it, took out the note, and on it was a short message of very valuable meaning. It read, "This too shall pass." As he read the sentence, he became very still. "This too shall pass." And it passed. Everything passes. Nothing is permanent in this world. The enemies who had been pursuing him must have gotten lost in the forest, must have taken a wrong path. After a while, he could no longer hear the sounds of their hooves. The king felt great gratitude to his servant and to that unknown mystic. These words had worked like a miracle. He folded the note again, put it back into the ring. He gathered his troops around him again and reclaimed his kingdom. And the day he victoriously re-entered his capital was celebrated grandly throughout the city, with music and dancing. He was very proud of himself. The old man walked beside his chariot. He said, "Now is the right moment again. Look at the message again." "What do you mean?" said the king. "Now I am victorious. The people are celebrating me. I am not in despair; I am not in a hopeless situation." "Listen to me," said the old man. "This is what the saint told me then: this message is not only for times of despair; it is also for times of joy. It's not just for when you're a loser. It is also true when you are victors; not only when you are last, but also when you are first." The king opened his ring and read the message, "This too shall pass." And suddenly the same peace, the same silence came over him - in the midst of the crowd that was rejoicing, celebrating and dancing. His pride, his ego were gone. Everything passes. He asked his old servant to come into his carriage and sit beside him. He asked him, "Is there anything else? Everything passes... Your message has helped me immensely." The old man said, "The third thing the wise man told me then was, "Remember that everything passes. Only you remain, you remain eternally as a witness."" [2]

All moments in life are precious. The difficult ones promote our growth and personal development if we let them. The good moments will also pass, so we should appreciate them in their uniqueness. It is important to accept that nothing can be held on to, that panta rhei applies.

What we should not do, however, is feed our monsters. Someone was kind enough to make a transcript of this wonderful narration in Ajahn Brahm's version from his Friday lectures. It is exactly the version in which I first heard it, delivered in his special way, which is a treat in itself:

"So if you're sitting comfortably, I will tell you the story. A long time ago, in one of those times when there were palaces, not with politicians and dictators, but real emperors. Emperors who were there because they were smart, they were wise, they were strong and very effective rulers. And it just happened that the emperor was away on some sort of business. And in his absence, a monster came in. It was a demon. Ugly, frightening, terrifying. And because this monster was so frightening, all of the soldiers, guards and people who were supposed to stop visitors coming in at the wrong time - they froze in terror, allowing this monster to walk right into the centre of the palace, and sit on the Emperor's throne. And when that monster sat down on the Emperor's chair, that was going too far. So the guards came to their senses, said "Get out of here! You don't belong! Who do you think you are?! That is our Emperor's chair, you can't sit in there." And, at those few unkind words, and unkind deeds, that monster grew an inch bigger. More frightening, more smelly, and more offensive. And that really upset all the people in the palace. They got out their swords, they clenched their fists, "if you don't move your butt, we'll carve it out with our swords, get out of here! Quick!" But every unkind word, unkind deed, even unkind thought, the monster grew an inch bigger every time, more ugly, more stinky, and the language got worse. And this had been going on a long time, when eventually the Emperor came back. And he came back into his palace, into his throne hall, and he saw this incredibly big, frightening monster there. It was so big; it took up most of the throne room. Huge. Talk about fat and obese. That monster, I've got nothing on that monster. The only reason I'm putting on weight by the way is because Buddhism is expanding, so am I. Anyway, back to the monster. This was one fat monster. And, he was so ugly, I mean really frightening, as I said in the story, even the great Steven Spielberg, with all the resources of Dreamworks, could not manufacture something so frightening. I've never seen Alien. But people say that's the most frightening monster in the movies. Is it? I don't know, but this monster was a hundred times as frightening as the Alien. It was terrifying. And as for the stench, coming off this monster, it smelled so bad that the maggots crawling over his body threw up - they were sick. They vomited. And the language, the language of this monster was worse, much worse, than you'd hear in Northbridge after the West Coast Eagles (an Australian football club) got beaten. It was one very sick monster. But, that Emperor, the reason he was the Emperor, was because of his great wisdom. He saw that terrifying, huge, stinky monster, and understood what to do. He said the wonderful word "welcome". Welcome monster. Thank you for coming. And at that, the monster grew an inch smaller. Less ugly, the maggots stopped throwing up, and his language got better. And the people around realized their mistakes. Instead of saying "get out", and getting angry, they started being kind to the monster. Welcome, you want something to eat? How about a pizza? Monster size. About three or four of them, got on the monster's feet to give him a foot massage. You've had a foot massage? Oh it's so rare getting a foot massage if you're a monster. That monster - "ooh, just over there a bit, ooh that's just right, there. "And they gave him cups of tea as well. They said "do you want a cup of tea or a cup of coffee? You know we have; we have Dilmar, from Sri Lanka. We have peppermint, it's good for your health. "And there were ... you know one lump or two of honey. They were so kind to that monster. And every kind act, word or thought, the monster grew an inch smaller, less ugly, less smelly, less offensive. And soon that monster was back to the size when he first came in. They didn't stop there. They carried on with their kindness so much, that soon that monster was so small, that one more act of kindness, and the monster vanished completely away. And that's how the monster was removed from the Emperor's palace. Not with "get out of here, you don't belong." But "welcome, thank you for coming. What can I do for you?" The Buddha told that story, that's a real story, from the Uddana in the Tipitaka. Only I added in a few details like the pizza, that wasn't [in the original] ... same for the foot massage, I added that. But, the essence is there. The anger ... and the Buddha said, to the monks, he said, we call that an Anger-Eating Demon. And when I first read that I thought "wow". That's a powerful message, anger-eating demon. You give them anger, that's what they eat. That's what they grow with. That's how they become more powerful. That's what makes them bigger, stronger and more negative. They feed off your ill-will. And I've seen that so often, you know with people I've looked at and worked with. You give them the problem - anger, "get out of here, you don't belong." [3]

Let's be mindful of what we nurture in our lives and what it looks like within ourselves:

"An old man was sitting outside the gates of a city. All the people going into the city passed him. A stranger stopped and asked the old man:

"I'm sure you can tell me what the people in this town are like?"
The old man looked at him kindly, "What were they like where you were last?" "Friendly, helpful and generous. Very pleasant people." the stranger replied. "That's just how they are in this town!" This pleased the stranger and with a smile he walked through the gate.

Later, another stranger came to the old man. "Tell me old man, what are the people like in this town?" The old man asked him too, "What were they like where you were last?" "Terrible! Unkind and arrogant." The old man replied, "I'm afraid they're like that in this town, too!""[4]

Attitude toward things is everything. But we must be careful of our attitude. It's amazing what we think we know. For example, what is good for us... If you have ever wished for something (job, relationship, etc.) but it turned out to be a complete disaster, you might have guessed it - there is a story about this too:

In a village in China, not quite small, but not big either, there lived a farmer - not poor, but not rich either, not very old, but not young anymore either, he had a horse. And because he was the only farmer in the village who had a horse, the people in the village said:

"Oh, such a beautiful horse is he lucky!"
And the farmer replied, "Who knows?!"

One day, an ordinary day, no one knows why, the farmer's horse broke out of its paddock and ran away. The farmer saw it galloping away, but he could not catch it. In the evening, the people of the village stood at the fence of the empty paddock, some grinning a little gleefully, and said:

"Oh the poor farmer, now his only horse has run away. Now he has no horse, poor man!"
The farmer probably heard this and just muttered, "Who knows?!"

A few days later, in the morning, in the farmer's paddock, the beautiful horse was seen chasing back and forth in play with a wild mare: she had followed him from the mountains. Great was the envy of the neighbors, who said:

 "Oh, how lucky he is, the farmer!"
But the farmer just said, "Who knows?!"

Then one fine day in summer, the farmer's only son got on the horse to ride it. Soon he was no longer alone, half the village was watching as he rode proudly on the beautiful horse. "Aah, how good he has it!"

But suddenly the horse spooked, reared up and the son, the only son of the farmer fell down and broke his leg, in many small pieces, up to the hip. And the neighbors cried out and said:

"Oh, the poor farmer, his only son! We wonder if he'll ever be able to walk properly again? Such bad luck!"
But the farmer just said, "Who knows?!"

Sometime later, the whole village was startled out of sleep when, towards morning, a wild clatter ran through the streets. The soldiers of the ruler came riding into the village and took all the boys and men out of bed to take them to war. The farmer's son could not go with them. And many a one sat at home and said:

"How lucky is he!"
But the farmer only muttered, "Who knows?!"[5]

We really don't know much, even frighteningly little, about ourselves (even if it seems quite different). This is not a story now, but a quote from Gerhard Roth in "Why it is so difficult to change yourself and others:" [6]

"This book was about a sober look at the possibilities and the limits of human changeability. This was done from the point of view of empirical-experimental psychology and brain research, which go hand in hand here. [...] First, we humans have little insight into what actually drives us [the unconscious], and second, by the time we finally have clear objectives as later adolescents and as adults, too much has already gone on in our personalities for us to be great change makers in our own right. This realization may be painful or offensive to our self-image, but life wisdom and science tell us that, as a rule, one needs outside help and impetus for major changes. [...] [And] actually, each of us knows this: words alone don't move anything, they have to appeal to emotions and motives of the one we want to change. This is not difficult with consciousness-led events on the upper limbic level, but, as heard, only of relatively small effect. We can only achieve stronger changes if we also reach the unconscious motives. [And this quickly comes up against limits, because contrary to Freud's conviction,] the unconscious cannot be made conscious, i.e., put into images and words, since it has no "format capable of being conscious." We can only ever gain indirect and generally unreliable knowledge of that which drives people unconsciously, and of which they themselves know nothing directly! [...] For the personality diagnostics, but also for the everyday contact with people this means: What a person communicates to us is - even if it is not an outright lie - always only a communication about the subjective view of oneself and the world, into which momentary feelings, memories, experiences, expectations and assumptions enter, especially with regard to what the interlocutor probably wants to hear or what is advantageous for oneself. It is never a reliable representation of the entire personality, because the unconscious, but also the current preconscious (i.e. the just not conscious contents of the long-term memory) are not accessible to the person giving information. The contents of the long-term memory are constantly rewritten "as needed", and memories cannot deliver objective reports! [...] People know themselves much less than a trained diagnostician (and sometimes a partner or friend) does."

So, that's it, we are alien-programmed zombies, not appreciably changeable, with whom no flower pot can be won. Total zero checkers who, thanks to many repression and justification mechanisms, nevertheless think they are great a priori.

There is nothing wise about this. Except to admit it to ourselves. Our ego is truly big, and obstructive. What is needed is mindfulness to see, humility to accept what we see, and expertise to understand it. Specifically, the psychological expertise is necessary. However, psychology should not become an end in itself (as it is often seen on Insta), but should be more like politics properly understood: it should create a framework in which good life is really possible. No more and no less.

Nevertheless, this knowledge is indispensable. Because let's face it, you have to take care of your own shit, and often diagnosticians are at the level of their studies, their "faith" school, and simply don't know many new publications that don't come with it.

Why do you need that? You can do without it, but it's like living in the matrix. The other day I tried to explain a certain behavior with the approach of codependency to someone without any psychological knowledge. The reaction was: "I don't believe that", "That's not logical".

Well, but anyway it was still there and the driving force of all the behavior mentioned by the person. Welcome to the power of the unconscious. How are you going to change something you don't recognize and understand?

Even if you understand the mechanisms, change is not easy and permanent, and it takes a lot of effort to achieve.

"So a consensus between unconscious motives and conscious goals is essential for longer-term change."[7]

And most importantly, you must act in such a way that the desired success can occur in the first place. There is a wonderful story about the lottery ticket:

"Moshe struggled with the world and fate - and complained to God:

"Lord, why are you so cruel? I have always been a good servant. You have taken everything from me. If you exist, show me that you are a good God - and let me win the lottery once."

Nothing happens. The next day Moshe prays again, nothing happens. He prays for a lottery win every day from then on - for a whole year. Then, finally, the hoped-for miracle happens, the heavens above him open and a deep voice speaks,

"Moshe, I have had to listen to your lament for a year, now, please, give me a chance - and finally buy a lottery ticket!"" [8]

If we supposedly want something, but do not act on it, everything we know and want is of no use. But it is also important for a happy life to be grateful for what we already have:

"A man once came to a Jewish rabbi complaining about the cramped conditions in his apartment. For him and his wife and the 5 children and the parents-in-law it was all too cramped and now relatives had announced themselves, there was simply no room. The rabbi asked: and do you also have animals? Yes, a goat and some chickens. Then take the chickens into the apartment and come back in a week. The man came back and was in despair: the chickens kept running between the people's feet or fluttering excitedly around the apartment, and the family suffered a lot. Well, said the rabbi, then take now the goat into the house.

The man tried to resist, but the rabbi was adamant. After this second week, the man was at his wits' end and threw himself before the rabbi, almost crying: the goat was disturbing everywhere, taking up a lot of space, and then the stench! Well, said the rabbi, then take the goat and the chickens back to the stable and come back in a week. No sooner said than done, a week later a happy man stood before the rabbi: we all have plenty of room, even the relatives, we get along well, and the horrible goat smell is gone, it smells like fresh hay or flowers or food. There you go, smiled the rabbi, go and rejoice in your beautiful home."[9]

The Stoics already practiced this exercise, namely to imagine losing something you already own (e.g. house, partner, children, wealth, health). Psychologically, it hurts us more to lose something we already have than it makes us happy to gain something new. That is why this exercise is so effective, and the Jewish joke proves it. Suddenly the apartment is quite nice just the way it is. With no goats inside.

In fact, if you cannot enjoy what you already have, then no matter what you may have, it will never be enough. This is also a matter of attitude and practice. A good practice is also to regularly reflect on what you are grateful for and to trace and savor this feeling.

But what to do when obviously bad things happen to you or are done to you? For this, there is the story from "The cow that cried - Buddhist stories about the path to happiness" by Ajahn Brahm with the beautiful title:

A truckload of crap

There are always unpleasant things in life - such as coming last in your class. Something like that can come over anyone. The only difference between a happy person and a depressed person is their reaction to adversity.

Now imagine that you've spent a wonderfully relaxing afternoon at the beach with a friend. And when you get home, you discover that someone has dumped a truckload of manure right outside your front door. Here's what you should know about this pile of manure:

You did not order it. It is not your fault. You're stuck with it now. No one saw who dumped it, so you can't ask anyone to take it away. He is filthy, disgusting, and nasty. His stench slowly permeates your entire house and is so unbearable that you could puke.

In this metaphor, the wagon load of dung represents all the traumatic experiences that life dumps on us. Just like the dung load, there are three things we need to know about the disaster in our lives:

We didn't order them. We ask, "Why me?"
We have them by the neck. No one, not even our best friends, can take them away from us (although they may try).
It is horrible, such a destroyer of our happiness that the pain fills our whole life. It is simply unbearable.

When you have a truckload of crap like that on your hands, there are two ways to respond. The first is to carry the crap around with us. We put some of it in our pockets and under our shirts. Yes, we even pour some of it down our pants. And then when we walk around with this crap, we find that we lose a lot of friends! Even the best of friends don't seem to show up that often anymore.

"Carrying the crap around" is a metaphor for sinking into depression, negative thoughts or anger. It's a perfectly natural reaction to adversity in life. But we lose a lot of friends, and it's perfectly understandable that they don't want to have much to do with us anymore if we're constantly walking around like seven days of rain. What's worse, the dung heap doesn't get cleared away in the process, but matures comfortably, so that its stench becomes more and more unbearable.

Fortunately, there is a second way. When someone dumps a truckload of manure on our doorstep, we let out a sigh and get to work. Wheelbarrow, pitchfork and spade are brought out. We shovel the manure into the wheelbarrow, drive it behind the house, and bury the stuff in the garden. It's exhausting and tiring work, but we know we have no other choice. Sometimes we only manage half a wheelbarrow a day. But we do something about the problem instead of dwelling on it until we finally end up in depression. Day in and day out, we load manure into the wheelbarrow, and every day the pile gets a little smaller.

Sometimes it takes us several years, but eventually there comes a morning when the pile of manure in front of the house is completely gone. Moreover, in the meantime, a true miracle has occurred in another part of our garden. The flowers are unfolding to their fullest splendor, and their fragrance fills the whole area, so that neighbors and even passersby begin to smile with joy. The fruit tree in the corner almost topples over, so richly blessed is it with tasty fruit. It bears so many that we can give our neighbors and even passers-by some of these miracle fruits.

"Digging in the dung," is also a metaphor. With it we welcome the mischief as fertilizer of life. We already have to do the work on our own, no one can help us. But if we dig the dung into the garden of our heart day in and day out, we can slowly remove the mountain of pain.

Maybe it will take us years, but the morning will come when we no longer see the pain in our lives and realize that a miracle has taken place in our hearts. Flowers of goodness are in full bloom. The fragrance of love fills the environment, our neighbors, our relationships, and even the people who pass by the garden. Then the tree of wisdom in the corner bends down to us, overloaded with the sweet insights into the nature of life. We distribute these delicious fruits generously, and even the casual passerby gets some, even if we didn't intend it.

When we have experienced the pain of tragedy, learned its lesson, and planted our garden, we can embrace each other in great tragedies and simply say, "I know." And the other person will understand that we really understand him. Compassion kicks in. We show him the wheelbarrow, the pitchfork, the spade, and encourage him to have boundless zeal. However, we could not possibly help this person if we had not tilled our own garden before.

I have met numerous monks who are great at meditation, facing adversity peacefully, calmly and serenely. But only a few of them have become great teachers. I have often wondered why that is. Today I believe that those monks who had it relatively easy and only had to clear away and dig in small piles of dung did not become teachers. But those who faced particularly great difficulties, who quietly cleared away the dung and were rewarded with a fertile garden, turned out to be the great teachers. All the monks were wise, serene, cheerful and full of compassion, but those with the bigger piles of dung had more to share with the world. At the doorstep of my teacher Ajahn Chah, for me the greatest teacher of all, dung heaps of unimaginable proportions were probably dumped in the past.

The moral of this story might be this: If you want to serve the world, to follow the path of compassion, then when faced with the next tragedy in your life, you might want to say, "Why, hello! Finally, more fertilizer for my garden!"[10]

How do I deal with it? Do I meet things at eye level and look for solutions that turn the bad into good, or do I let myself become a victim, seeing only the bad?

It is fatal to lose eye level, especially in relationships. It is fatal to forget that one is an adult and certainly not helpless. As Viktor Frankl said so beautifully, "I don't have to take everything from myself."

It is fatal to bend and lose your peace of mind. It is fatal not to call a spade a spade:

"Many years ago there lived an emperor. He thought so tremendously of new clothes that he spent all his money on this splendor. He did not care for his soldiers, did not attend to the affairs of state, and did not love to go into the forest except to show off his new clothes. He had his own skirt for every hour of the day, and people talked behind closed doors, "The emperor is already taking his wardrobe out again!"

In the great city where the emperor lived, things were lively. Many strangers arrived every day, and one day two impostors also came. They pretended to be weavers and said that they could weave the most beautiful cloth in the world. The clothes made of the fabric would not only be unusually beautiful, they would also have a wonderful property. They would be invisible to anyone who was no good at his job or simply stupid.

"These must be splendid clothes indeed," the emperor thought to himself. "If I had them, I could also learn which men in my kingdom are no good. I could distinguish the clever from the stupid! Yes, this cloth must be woven for me at once!"

He gave the two swindlers a lot of money to start their work. They also set up two looms and pretended to work. But there was not the slightest thing on the looms. Nevertheless, the two men demanded the finest silk and the most magnificent gold. But they put this into their own pockets and worked on the empty looms until late at night.

"Now I would like to know how far they have come with the fabric," thought the emperor. But he was a little afraid, since good-for-nothings and fools should not be able to see the weaving work. Although the emperor believed that he had nothing to fear for himself, he wanted to send someone else first. All the people in the whole city knew the power of the cloth, and all were eager to see how bad or stupid the neighbors were.

"I will send my old, honest minister to the weavers," said the emperor. "He can best judge what is going on, for he has sense. And no one performs his office better than he!" Now the old, good minister went into the hall where the two swindlers were working at the empty looms. "God preserve us!" thought the old minister, widening his eyes. "I can't catch a glimpse of anything!" But he didn't let on.

The swindlers asked him to come closer and asked if it was not a pretty pattern and beautiful colors. Then they pointed to the empty loom, and the poor minister could not believe his eyes. He could see nothing, for there was nothing there. "Lord," he thought, "am I one of the stupid ones? I never thought so, and no man must know it!"

"Well, you don't say anything?" asked one of the weavers. "Oh, it's wonderful to look at!" replied the old minister, looking inquiringly through his glasses. "That pattern and those colors! - Yes, I will tell the emperor that I like it very much!" "Well, we're glad!" the weavers replied, and went on for a long time explaining the special colors and patterns. The old minister listened carefully so that he could tell everything when he came before the emperor again.

But now the swindlers demanded even more money, and in addition silk and gold for weaving. They put everything back into their own pockets and continued to work on the empty looms.

The emperor soon sent another capable statesman to see how the weaving was going. But he was just like the old minister. He looked and looked, but apart from the loom, there was nothing to be seen. "Isn't that a splendid and pretty piece of cloth?" asked the two swindlers. And they showed the statesman the splendid pattern that wasn't there at all. "Stupid I am not," thought the man. "So it is my good office to which I am unfit! But I don't want anyone to know that!" So the statesman praised the fabric that he could not see and expressed his delight at the beautiful colors and gorgeous pattern. "Yes, it is truly the best!" he said to the emperor.

All the people in the city spoke only of the magnificent fabric. That is why the emperor wanted to see it himself. The emperor immediately selected a whole crowd of outstanding men, including the old minister and the statesman. Then they went to the two impostors, who were weaving again, but without fiber and thread.

"Look," said the old minister "isn't it splendid?" And the weavers asked, "Will Your Majesty see what pattern, what colors?" Then they pointed to the empty loom, and explained the wonderful fabric in the most beautiful words.

"Oh dear," thought the emperor, "I can't see a thing! This is terrible! Am I stupid? Am I not fit for the office of emperor? What am I to do?" He thought for a moment and said, "Well, the fabric is very pretty and deserves my applause!" He nodded with satisfaction and looked at the empty loom from all sides. The whole entourage watched and rubbed their eyes, but everyone said the same thing as the emperor. In the end, they also advised the emperor to wear the miracle clothes for the first time at the great feast that was soon to come.

The whole night before the feast the cheaters were to be seen at their looms, so that one could also observe them quite well at their work. They pretended to take the cloth from the loom, they cut with big scissors in the air, they sewed with needles without thread and at last they said: "Look, now the clothes are ready!"

The emperor came with his most distinguished officials, and both impostors raised one arm just as if they were holding something. They said, "Your Majesty, here are the leggings. Here is the dress! And here is the coat! Everything is as light as cobwebs. You'd think you had nothing on your body, but that's just the beauty of it!"

"Yes," said all the officials, but they could see nothing, for there was nothing there. "Does Your Majesty now wish to take off the old clothes," asked the swindlers, "then let us put on the new clothes here in front of the big mirror!"

The emperor took off his clothes and the impostors posed as if they were going to put on him every piece of the new clothes. The emperor put up with it and turned and twisted in front of the mirror. "Wow, how splendidly the new clothes fit!" everyone exclaimed. "What patterns, what colors! This is a truly precious suit!" The emperor turned again in front of the mirror, for it should look as if he wanted to look at his clothes once more.

The chamberlains, who had the right to carry the coat train, now reached their hands to the floor. They pretended to pick up the train, for they dared not let on. So the emperor then went out, and all the people in the street and in the windows said: "The emperor's new clothes are really incomparable! How beautiful the train is, and how well everything fits!"

No one wanted to let on that they saw nothing. For everyone was afraid of being called a good-for-nothing in his office or a fool. "But he's not wearing anything!" said a little child at last. "Don't listen to that!" said the father. But people were now whispering to each other what the child had said. Then suddenly all the people shouted, "But he's not wearing anything!" The emperor was deeply frightened, for he felt that it must be the truth. "Well," the emperor thought to himself, "it has happened, and I must now keep my composure and dignity." So the chamberlains continued to wear the invisible cloak until the feast was over.[11]

Not being congruent makes you a cripple. If you do not live in congruence with your boundaries, values and morals, you cannot be an upright person. However, you should not, because of misunderstood "authenticity," think to rub your opinion of everything and everyone in others' faces. Thus Rumi said so beautifully: "Before you speak, let your words pass through three gates. At the first gate ask, "Are they true?" At the second ask, "Are they necessary?" At the third gate ask, "Are they kind?"" - speak first then or keep silent.

When it comes to other people in your life, there is even more to consider. It's not hard to see that when it's good, it's good. It is only in difficulties and crises that you will realize your true friends. [12]

It is of enormous importance what kind of people you surround yourself with. Even the ancient Romans knew that you have to stay away from toxic, immoral and destructive people, otherwise you can only lose:

Phaedrus lamb and wolf

The wolf and the lamb had once come to the same river, attracted by thirst: Further up stood the wolf and far below the sheep. Driven by ravenous hunger, he brought a reason for a quarrel.

"Why," he said, "have you stirred up the water I am about to drink?" The wool bearer retorted, fearing:

"Please, tell me, how can I do what you're complaining about, Wolf? From you the water flows down to my throat."

Restrained by the forces of truth, he said, "Six months ago you insulted me."

Then the lamb replies, "I wasn't even born then."

"By Hercules," cried that one, "then your father has offended me;" so he rends the innocent lamb in unjust murder.

This fable is written because of those people who oppress innocent people for invented reasons. [13]

As you can see impressively, all talking and arguing is of no use. It is not rational and there is no good will. Just get out of there. It is necessary to recognize who disqualifies himself with his behavior in order to draw the consequences for himself without discussions. To put it bluntly, people can be wonderful and enriching, or they can be the biggest pests there are. If you are a good person in a toxic environment, you will be gnawed to the bone. Your goodness will not change the destructive person. Since being good is very costly, you must choose the people in your life very carefully.

It becomes even more costly to not know who you are and what you want, then others fill those gaps with their views and agendas, and these won't really be in your best interest or good for you:

The ugly duckling

Once upon a time there was a mother duck who was hatching her eggs. There were exactly seven eggs in her nest and the mother duck was already looking forward to her offspring. One day the time had finally come and six lively ducklings hatched out of the eggs. They were all beautiful and covered with a yellow, delicate feather fuzz. Only the seventh egg was still lying intact in its nest. It was larger than the other eggs and as much as the mother duck thought about it, she couldn't remember when she had actually laid it? Just as the mother duck was thinking about this again, the last egg cracked and out came a gray duckling that looked at its mother in wonder. The days flew by. The six ducklings grew up quickly and learned something new every day. Only the last and seventh duckling caused her worries. It was not only clumsy, but also very ugly. The animals on the farm mocked the gray duckling and no one wanted to play with him. The mother duck was also very worried and sadly lamented: "All my children are so pretty and clever, only the last duckling has turned out so ugly. Nobody wants to have anything to do with him and even the other animals avoid him." Nevertheless, the mother duck was also very fond of this duckling and so she tried to comfort it again and again. Then she spoke to it and asked it sadly, "My poor little duckling, why aren't you like your brothers and sisters? Why can't you be like them?" But no one knew the answer to this question. Neither the siblings nor the mother and certainly not the ugly duckling himself. Even the little ugly duckling did not miss the fact that he was different from his siblings and that no one on the farm wanted to have anything to do with him. It felt lonely, sad and left alone. At night, when his siblings and all the other animals on the farm slept peacefully, the little duckling cried secretly to himself and found no sleep. The weeks and months passed and his loneliness grew as much as the ridicule of the other animals on the farm. One morning, the little duckling had once again cried all night, and decided to simply run away. He could no longer bear the ridicule and scorn of the others.

On the farm the animals were still sleeping and the little duckling set off. It didn't take long and after a while he reached a small pond where two swans were swimming proudly and majestically. As much as the little duckling had wished for it, the two swans didn't know the answer to why it was so ugly? Sadly, it waddled on, while the two swans gave it a warning about the hunters, who had just taken up position around the water in the early morning. Sadly it waddled on and soon reached a lake. The sun was already a little higher, birds were chirping, and on the shore a few deer eyed the ugly duckling suspiciously. At the lake, the little duck asked all the animals if they had ever heard of a duckling with gray feathers. But wherever he asked, they all gave the duckling the same answer: "No, we've never heard of it, and we've never seen a duckling uglier than you!" Then a few big tears rolled down the little duckling's face and, sobbing sadly, he walked on until he finally reached the little house of an old farmer's wife. She was very old and her eyes were not the best anymore, so it was not surprising that the old woman thought the little duckling was a goose. While reaching for the duckling, she murmured softly to herself and said to herself, "Hmm, goose eggs are something fine. The best thing to do is to put you in a cage right now." From now on, every morning the old farmer's wife came to the duckling to see if it had already laid fresh goose eggs. But no matter how often the old farmer's wife looked, the little duckling just didn't lay any eggs. The other animals on the little farm did not miss the new guest either. The chicken of the farmer's wife already warned the little duckling and said: "Just see to it that you finally lay eggs, otherwise the old woman will possibly slaughter you in the end and you will end up as roast goose on her lunch table!" The house cat blasphemed hostilely hissing: "Hopefully you land soon in the roast tube, because something so ugly has never come under me!" The little duckling's heart sank, especially since the old lady had been fattening it up for a few days, so that it would grow fat and big. Full of despair, the little duckling thought about how it could escape its fate. One night, the farmer's wife had accidentally left the cage door open, and the little duck decided to escape! He ran as far and as fast as his little strength would allow, and when dawn came, he reached a thick thicket of reeds by a beautiful lake. In it it hid and came slowly again to the rest. It took a few days and the little duck settled down in the thick reeds of the lake. Here it was well hidden, no one could see it and food was abundant. But as much as it was protected here, with every day the loneliness hurt a little more and sadly it said to itself: "If nobody wants to love me, then I'll just stay here in my hiding place, where at least nothing can be done to me!

So the days and weeks passed and even our little duckling had finally found some peace. On a beautiful late summer day, the little duckling enjoyed the last warming rays of the sun and looked up to the sky, where he just saw a flock of white birds majestically passing by. With their yellow beaks and long narrow necks they looked beautiful and the little duck sighed sadly: "Just once, just once I would like to be so beautiful! Then I'm sure all the other animals will really love me for once!" Full of longing and melancholy, it looked after the proud and sublime birds until they disappeared on the distant horizon. While the little duckling still often had to think of the proud birds, the days passed and the food in the reeds became less and less. Winter had come over the land and one morning the lake with the reed belt had frozen over as well. Sad, lonely and hungry, the little duckling left its hiding place to look for food. But in the meantime it was so weakened by the long-lasting hunger that it sank exhausted to the ground and simply remained lying in the snow. But it was lucky! Shortly thereafter, a farmer came by and when he found the poor, half-starved animal, he took pity on it and said to himself: "I will take you with me. You are already half frozen and my children will surely feed you up and be happy about you!" Shortly after, the good man put the little duckling in his pocket and took it home. The children of the farmer lovingly took care of the little duckling and were happy every day when they saw how the duckling slowly regained its strength and grew bigger. Well cared for, fed and in the warmth of the farm, the duckling was able to survive the winter. In spring, the duckling had already grown so big that the farmer brought it back to the reed thicket. Happy and satisfied, it jumped into the water and spread its wings. It enjoyed the warm spring rays of the sun and stuck its head into the clear water of the lake full of high spirits. When it raised its head again and looked at the water, it paused in amazement: "Is that really me? Why have I changed so much?" Because what the once small, ugly duckling now saw was the reflection of itself. The reflection of a proud and beautiful swan! It also did not take long and the swans from the south also returned to their beloved lake. Shyly and still a bit afraid, the little duckling approached the swans and when they noticed the little duckling, they took it in their midst and said: "We are swans and you are one of us! Where have you been all this time?" With big astonished but happy eyes, the young swan looked at his new comrades and murmured, "That's a long and exciting story!"

From that day on, the young swan swam on the lake with all the other swans and was very happy and also the children, who had cared for him so lovingly during the winter, suddenly stood by the lake one day and shouted with joy: "Just look, just look! There is our little swan! Look how beautiful he has become! He really is the most beautiful of all!"[14]

You must know who you are, what you want, and be at peace within yourself, and choose your company wisely. I talked in my previous books about how significant it is to have a clear moral framework for yourself in order to live a good life. The following story teaches us that sometimes there are values for which ours must be bent. Or rather, subordinated to higher ones. If you decide this for yourself from the fullness of your heart, you will still remain at peace with yourself:

A young and an old monk make a pilgrimage. They come to a river with a strong current. There stands a young pretty woman who is obviously afraid to cross the river.

Without hesitation, the old monk goes to the woman, lifts her on his shoulders and carries her to the other shore. She thanks him and goes on her way. The two monks then continue their pilgrimage. Hours later, the young monk begins to criticize the other and angrily says:

"You know that as monks we are not allowed to touch women! How could you break that rule?"

The old monk, who had carried the woman across the river, listens calmly to the other's reproaches. Then he answers:

"I left that woman on the riverbank hours ago - why are you still carrying her around?"

And as you can see in this story, if it is perfectly clear to you what you did and why, and can have your peace with it, it doesn't matter at all what others think about it.
They will always have an opinion (although not as often as you think, you are not so exciting that others would constantly think about you). Except for a selected and tested group of people whose opinions really matter to you, you shouldn't care about the opinions of other people. There is, of course, a wonderful story about this as well:

On a hot summer day, in the blazing midday heat, a father, his son and a donkey were walking through the dusty alleys of a small town in the Orient.

The father sat on the donkey and the boy walked beside him. Then a veiled woman passed by, shook her head uncomprehendingly and said:

"The poor boy. He can hardly keep up the pace of the donkey with his short legs. How can a father be so heartless and sit lazily on the donkey while his boy is all exhausted from walking."

The father, ashamed when he heard these words, dismounted and put his son on the donkey. Soon after, an elderly man came along the way. When he saw the travelers, he shouted angrily:

"What impertinence. There the brat sits on the donkey while his poor old father walks along beside him."

This pained the boy, who loved his father, and he immediately asked him to sit behind him on the donkey.

The next thing I knew, a hiker came by and got indignant at the top of his voice:

"Has anyone seen anything like this? What a cruelty to animals! The poor donkey's back is already sagging completely and these two lazy bums are resting on it."

These words also struck them both deeply. And so father and son got down from the donkey, took the animal in the middle and walked beside it on the right and left. It wasn't long before a stranger was making fun of her:

"What a waste! What is the use of taking the donkey for a walk if it is good for nothing and does not even carry one of you?"

Thereupon the father shook his head, gave the donkey a handful of straw and said to his son:

"No matter what we do, there's always someone who doesn't like it. I guess we have to decide for ourselves what is right for us." (after Nasreddin Hodja)

Understood? Sometimes, again, we ourselves are not clear how to deal with the world's problems. Thanks to global networking and markets, 24-hour news and the Internet, we are constantly confronted with the bad news and problems of the whole world, around the clock. As soon as we consume something, to some extent we become complicit in the exploitation of humans, animals and the planet. We feel responsible and in charge and at the same time helpless, because there are so overwhelmingly big problems, and you as a small consumer without power and influence and money to buy the policies you want, suspect very well that you can only have a very small global impact. The following story is meant to comfort you: in that even though you may not be able to save the whole world, you actually do have a big impact individually. That's something.

The starfish

As an elderly man was walking along the beach at sunset, he saw a young man in front of him picking up starfish and throwing them into the sea. After catching up with him, he asked him why he was doing that. The answer was that the stranded starfish would die if they remained here until sunrise.

"But the beach is many miles long and thousands of starfish lie here," the old man replied, "So what difference does it make if you struggle?"

The young man looked at the starfish in his hand and tossed it into the waves. Then he said, "It makes a difference to this one!"

And for this one, it makes a really very big difference. What also makes a big difference is how you look at things in life, especially the supposedly small things:

The old wise woman and the lucky beans

A very old, wise woman never left her house without first taking a handful of beans. She did not do this to chew the beans on the way.
No, she took the beans with her so that she could better count the beautiful moments in life.
For every little thing she experienced during the day - for example, a cheerful chat on the street, a delicious-smelling loaf of bread, a

moment of silence, someone's laughter, a touch of the heart, a shady spot in the midday heat, the chirping of a bird - for everything that delighted the senses and the heart, she let a bean move from her right jacket pocket to her left.

Sometimes there were two or three beans that changed places at once.

In the evening, the wise woman sat at home by the fireplace and counted the lucky beans from her left jacket pocket. She celebrated these minutes. In this way, she reminded herself of how many beautiful things had happened to her that day and rejoiced in them.

Even on the evenings when she counted only one bean, every day was a happy day for her - it had been worth living. (Author unknown) [15]

Gratitude is the key to everything. It lifts your spirits, makes you appreciate more and enjoy what you already have. You can feel gratitude and joy even in hard times, if you allow it and don't lose sight of the little moments and things. Gratitude can help you bring light back into the darkness. What can you start to be grateful for?

Very easy: "When you awake in the morning, remember what a delicious treasure it is to be able to live, to breathe, and to rejoice." - Marcus Aurelius. For what it's worth, the sunrises, the crispness of the morning and the chirping of the birds alone are worth it, and there's so much more....

If you can stay with yourself, what more do you want: "There is a beautiful sentence by Tranxu, a great Chinese sage, which I have memorized well. It reads. 'If the archer shoots without wanting to win a special prize, he can develop all his art; if he shoots to win a bronze medal, he begins to get restless; if he shoots for the first prize, he becomes blind, sees two targets and loses his temper. His skill is the same, but the prize splits him. It is important to him! He thinks more about winning than shooting, and the compulsion to win weakens him.' Doesn't this image apply to most people?"[16]

WHAT
I HAVE LEARNED
SO FAR

1. All the problems in the world are rooted in the fact that we don't want to see ourselves and our emotions.... This then leads to chronic stress, conflicts, addictive behavior and downward spirals through repression and thus lasts virtually forever, because the actual problem is not addressed at any time: we are emotionally out of control children in fancy adult suits.

2. And by everyone, I really mean everyone. All the destruction you can see on the planet, the violence, the wars, the oppression is the result of the action of our little ego that wants to convince us that we are better and more entitled than the others, because we can't bear to see ourselves as we really are. We'd rather make the others feel bad, that makes us feel good.

3. People change at most through pain (in very high doses, through trauma or strokes of fate), and some do not change even then. Certainly not by telling them something well argued. So save your spit.

4. People usually don't want to change because it's painful, and repression is so wonderfully convenient and all-powerful. One prefers to stay with the diffuse chronic pain and latent dissatisfaction and tension. You hardly notice them anymore, because you don't feel yourself anyway.

5. Consider how hard it is to change yourself. The same applies to you as above. That is why therapy may be of no use if it remains only on the cognitive level. You need to process it emotionally, feel and experience the new, break behavioral patterns and habits, feel it deep into the unconscious and the cells, so that a profound change can take place.[17]

6. True change is only accomplished when it feels effortless and inner peace takes hold, when not only your behavior but your

personality changes. Everything else is just redecorating and usually doesn't last. The new must become an experienced and lived part of who you are.

7. Lasting change clearly only works from within. True to the motto: Happiness is an inside job.

8. Consequently, change only works if you don't attach it to anything outside, or cling to things, as the Buddhists put it. Think of the story of the archer in the chapter before.

9. If it costs your inner peace, it is too expensive. Inner peace, however, seems to be a rare phenomenon.

10. If you could not be absolutely alone with yourself, you are not free. Even among people, life is quite lonely. Accept that. Learn to be good with yourself alone instead of lonely. Remember, the only person who will certainly accompany you until death is yourself. With the others it is uncertain. It is better to be alone than in bad company. That costs way too much.

11. Be kind to yourself, don't slow yourself down. "Life shrinks or expands in proportion to our courage." -Anais Nin

12. But it is still the case that without love everything is nothing. However, love and lived closeness certainly brings vulnerability and thus pain into your life. You cannot be at a distance and love. That is hollow; there is then no life in it.

13. Unconditional love should be given by parents. Among adults, this cannot be made up and leads to strange assumptions, such as these "take me as I am (no matter how many maturity deficits and unresolved problems I have)."

That doesn't really sound promising, does it? Responsibility is borne by each one for himself.

14. Responsibility is the sine qua non. If you do not take responsibility for your life and your actions, you have not arrived at adulthood. Mirriam Prieß aptly describes it repeatedly in her books: "There is no adult reason to remain in the sorrow of past relationships. There is no reason to hold on to people, situations or relationships, both professionally and privately, that harm us and in which we are not happy. There is no basis for "not managing to leave, or not managing to stay at eye level in a clarifying way." Feeling victimized as an adult can only happen if we don't want to leave the child level. A child is a victim - an adult is always a perpetrator. As long as we are not willing to acknowledge this, we have not yet left our parental home and as a childlike adult we wait helplessly as in vain for the next reparation from our environment.
In the end, the real healing lies not in the recognition of the childish injury, but in the willingness, in this recognition, to renounce childhood for good and to leave the childish level forever." [18]

15. Since loving and being altruistic is very costly, you should choose the people to whom you give this very carefully.

16. Unfortunately, you can be too nice, too generous, too giving and too loving... You will no longer be appreciated for it, let alone get the same back. At most, demanding reproaches if you reduce or stop this behavior due to one-sidedness.

17. People respond to you within their own limitations and capabilities. Therefore, stop speaking to the mind of the ignorant one.

18. How a person judges you usually says more about them than you. Don't give much to criticism. Usually criticism is just useless and crap, and rarely with any real intention of lovingly pointing out your weaknesses to help you to be a better person. Rarely is it about telling you something unpleasant, but which is truly in your best interest, without judging or devaluing you. Guard the handful of people who give you this kind of feedback like true treasures, because they are your real friends. Only give a damn about your own opinion and that of these select and proven individuals. It is best to ignore the criticism of others, which is usually intended simply to belittle you, and which projects the complexes and deficiencies of others onto you so that they can feel better about themselves.

19. This usually works out quite well if you really don't care about the opinion of others. Really don't care from the bottom of your heart. And this not because you are a pretentious arrogant fop, but because you really know yourself so well that you can confidently rest within yourself. Because you do not deny your shadows, but are clearly in contact with yourself, but also do not minimize your own light in order to please anyone or not to alienate people in your environment. If this should be "necessary", you are totally wrong there anyway. Pay close attention to who and what you surround yourself with, because:

20. Environment always wins. Pay close attention to what kind of people you let into your life, what kind of content you consume (TV, online, news, social media), what you basically let into your mind and body.

21. Compassion is better than empathy because the latter draws you into strong feelings (of others) and then limits your ability to act. Compassion enables you to take part in the difficult experience of the other person without being

emotionally involved, which gives you a completely different view and room for maneuver. In too strong feelings you should refrain from making important long-term decisions, no matter whether these feelings are very bad or very good. Exuberance is also not a good advisor.

22. You can unfortunately have too much compassion and understanding, and thereby put up with the bad behavior of another person, because you can bear it and understand the troubles of the other. Unfortunately, by doing so, you "teach" less developed and less reflective specimens only that they can do it with you. With all understanding: be glad that this makes you calmer and does not bring additional stress into the system, this in itself can be a relief. But: show clear boundaries and demand appropriate and decent behavior towards you. You are otherwise teaching people that they can treat you badly and get away with it.

23. If a person disqualifies himself by his behavior, do not stop him and simply throw him out of the game. This will save a lot of suffering, grief and time, and above all, energy that you could usefully put into other people and things that deserve it. Maya Angelou said it so well, "When someone shows you who they are, believe them the first time." Believe her.

24. This brings us to the subject of personal boundaries. Which, it seems to me, is a misunderstood major construction site for many people. The best definition of a personal boundary is from Townsend and Cloud: "Remember that the boundary is always about you, not about others. You are not asking your partner to do anything - not even to respect your boundaries, [that's the point:]. You are the one who sets the boundaries to show what you will and will not do. Only this kind of limitation is enforceable because you yourself are in control. With your behavior, you [...] allow your partner to take

responsibility for his behavior." [19] This means that it is up to you whether you protect the boundaries. And it means that when in doubt, you yourself are not afraid of the ultimate consequence: a possible end to the relationship.

The last inner conflict is: fear of abandonment versus protection of one's boundaries, which is actually more important, because we fall apart when we don't respect our own boundaries and ourselves....

When the fear of being abandoned gets the upper hand, the partner has a free hand to shit on us and do whatever he pleases (and he's usually good at recognizing just that and pushing it to the max). Of course, this applies to relationships other than couples as well, but it is here that the issue of boundaries becomes most apparent. If you deny yourself and let yourself down by putting up with everything, you will hate yourself for putting up with it and the person who does it. This will certainly not lead to anything good.

25. It is imperative that you have clear moral principles and values to guide your life, because these give you support and the comfort of being able to look yourself in the eye in the mirror at night. In difficult times and relationships, they help you protect your boundaries and not throw yourself away, but stand up for yourself and do and demand what is right. (I write about this in more detail in the book Radical Practice Peace of Mind). You must have expectations and standards that are non-negotiable. It is up to you to match whether your counterpart shares them and lives up to them. It is not your job to educate adult people. You can in no way make people who are not like that be like that.

26. Likewise, in a toxic environment, you cannot heal. You are not a Zen monk, with unwavering equanimity, so don't lie to yourself and stop asking inhuman things of yourself. Also,

please note that Zen monks do not have, and certainly do not have toxic, relationship partners. Instead, surrounded by morally like-minded and compassionate people, they usually live in the most beautiful natural environment and lead a regulated and healthy life. Do you notice anything?

27. Couple relationships:

This closest relationship is the full participation in the conscious and repressed unconscious problems and however (possibly dysfunctional or even toxic) other existing relationships of the other person, e.g. family, friends, etc., which are still ongoing and will also have an impact on you.

The common thing is, many things are only triggered by the increasing commitment, because then the behavior patterns from childhood and any failed relationships that are deeply imprinted under "love" come into play. Unconsciously, we always re-enact the closest relationships we "learned" early on, because no matter how objectively awful and unloving it may have been, that is what has stuck with us under "love." Since it's unconscious, it sort of jumps on automatically when it gets "serious enough." Even if you have rationally recognized patterns, it is still not enough for them to stop kicking in. When in love, we are all idiots in a special way, because we like to see things that are not there, but we wish they were and would like them to be, and also still believe what the other person tells us about himself. The sad truth is: even if he is not lying to you, his ego is not able to see him himself. Don't worry; it is the same way with you.

So one fantasy meets another and it's only in the relationship that it becomes apparent what unresolved issues and maturity deficits have actually met.

The greatest gift you can give yourself (and also your partner)

- you will be happier and your partner will simply suffer less from you - is to accept your more or less obvious (addictive) problems, to admit to yourself your repression and escape from difficult emotions and to take a close look at them, because they need to be worked on so that you can really become the person your own little ego wrongly thinks you are.

You need to confront yourself with your pain, difficult emotions and fears so that you can grow in your humanity and have a good and loving relationship. Your partner needs to strive for this for themselves as well, because it takes two like-minded people to have a relationship. (How you can do this, and work with your emotions, and shape your relationships, I describe in detail in: "Stay away from idiots")

A relationship certainly does not need anyone who brings you suffering and pain and drama, and thinks that you should suffer and bear his deficits in the "name of love". If you recognize yourself, and can function as far as possible without your own repression, then you also see much more clearly how your counterpart really is. Here applies: choose wisely!

The ancient Greeks said that you enter into relationships because it speeds up recognition, in a relationship you can't permanently pretend to be someone you might like to be, but factually are not. The truth, since it can't be hidden from the other person forever, spills out no matter what, and the other person lets you know it.... So look sincerely at your own behavior, which you show, and ask yourself: is this how the person behaves who I think I am/who I want to be? Yes it is endless work, and no one says it is easy - but it is worth it. **Not just** for the relationship, but for yourself. Especially for yourself.

28. On narcissistic/ toxic relationships:

If you should already detect "smoke" at the beginning: walk away. In no case go deeper in to see if it really burns or how much.

For those who have already fallen into the trap: Don't lose time, energy, health and love that you could give to people who would appreciate it. Acknowledge that you are in such a relationship, accept it as fact/reality, and draw the consequences. Leave. This person is so disturbed; he can't and won't give you love, appreciation and affection. Go away. Do not think about it; do not try to understand the behavior. It is a mental disorder that involves antisocial, hurtful and inconsiderate behavior that is not treatable due to lack of insight/repression. This is not a mystery and really nothing new if you have been in it long enough. It's a waste of your precious life time to keep thinking about it. Recover from the massive stress, be good to yourself, protect your boundaries (preferably no contact, delete the person on social media, you have a right to forget) and be happy that this person is no longer a part of your life. Be happy to be free and be happy about your new and carefree life. For God's sake, don't ruminate about the relationship when it's over. Don't give even the slightest second to it. The past is dead. There is no point in thinking about it. Instead, dance on the tables, look forward to the good things to come and enjoy your life. No one will poison this one for you again...if you don't let them. Real joy is possible again, enjoy it.

29. Genuine joy, by the way, is only possible if you are not in a permanent state of alarm and your basic needs for security, predictability, belonging and autonomy are satisfied. You should also be well-rested and not hungry. Constant drama and a toxic environment that drags you down and weighs

you down because it constantly brings new problems and perceived guilt into your life is certainly not one of them. That's why point 20 is so elementarily important. It costs YOUR joy of life.

30. Being single says nothing about how you are in a couple relationship. It's just that other mechanisms kick in. You can be a happy single, and still find yourself in an unhappy relationship. Nevertheless, you should be a happy single, being good with yourself alone is the most important thing.

31. Dating: don't waste time worrying about what the other person thinks of you. Be yourself, in the long run there is nothing else anyway. Observe carefully: what kind of person is he, what kind of values does he have? Does he live them? What about him/her or this person's behavior will I find problematic in the long run? What is this person's environment and interpersonal contacts like? Am I really up for it? Does he/she take responsibility for his/her own life? If you are older than 13, you already know that responsibility and reliability and a clear moral backbone and loyalty are very very sexy. Please do not confuse problematic with interesting in any way. They are not the same thing.

32. Interaction with others:

Do not attach importance to being liked by others, otherwise you will become a people pleaser who is not taken seriously and who is also latently chronically angry because he does not get what he wants: real recognition and appreciation and no opportunity to do what he really wants. Do not confuse people pleasing with loyalty; the real one should belong to yourself and your partner, as the most important people in your life. Surprisingly many people pleasers neglect this in order to curry favor with strangers, to make an impression, and to be pleasing to others. In doing so, you let yourself down, and the person who is supposedly most important to you - because they obviously have to understand that you supposedly can't help it. This is really not at eye level, and not to have eye level in interpersonal contact is simply immature. Even just pragmatically, your partner is the person with whom you spend your life and most of your time - it would be healthy self-interest to give this relationship priority over everything else, because it has the most impact on you. Never mind what the neighbors think. Don't care about that, care about yourself, your loved ones and your home.

In dealing with others, you do not have to be an ace, of course; a cultivated and friendly approach should be a matter of course - even when dealing with your partner, by the way. As a principle, meet people friendly in the first contact, and then adapt to the counterpart. Then it's tit for tat. This way you avoid investing too much, and falling back into the role of putting up with everything to your detriment. Accept the following truth about interpersonal relationships: You are not a tomato soup, so that everyone likes you.

33. However, if you discover something beautiful about your counterpart, find something good, or particularly well done by him / her: In the name of God, say it out loud. We are far too stingy with compliments, and unnecessarily deprive ourselves of the joy of giving and receiving them. Friendly interaction and authentic appreciation is worth its weight in gold in interpersonal relationships.

34. Stay away from other people's problems, don't let them become yours. There are two levels to this. In the first one, you actively try to solve other people's problems for them by getting involved in things that are ultimately out of your control anyway (and you are much more than the people themselves actually affected by them), which is very pointless and costs you a lot of energy and your time. Examples: trying to influence someone to be more "sensible", e.g. not drinking,

not getting themselves into trouble all the time, not squandering their money; dealing with conflicts for third parties (keyword drama triangle), or doing tasks that people can very well do themselves, e.g. Hotel Mama with full service for stay-at-home etc. To avoid this, ask yourself: can I really influence this? (You can only really influence what depends on you all alone!). And second question: is it my responsibility? This refers to things YOU have done or omitted. Since with the omission the demarcation seems more difficult: it is not acceptable that you get yourself into trouble, or behave morally wrong to "help" someone, e.g. lie for a friend that he was with you, although he cheats on his wife at the time, or even put yourself in danger, or commit criminal acts. Anything that would lead to such things you must refrain from doing, because then there will be damage to you. This leads us to the second level: without you becoming active, the problems of others become part of your life: e.g. your partner taking out his stress at work on you, your neighbor regularly giving you whining tirades about his difficult life or illnesses or gossip about other people who are not present, the "overstrained" colleague dumping his work on you, or your friends and relatives trying to awaken feelings of guilt in you for something, so that you are available to them for their purposes. All these are not your problems, but those of other people. As a rule, you definitely can't help these people because they don't want to solve their problems at all, they want the drama and someone to jump around them and feel responsible for them.

Urgently check all stressful, difficult and critical situations in your life to see if they are really your construction site. If you have never done this consciously before, you will be amazed at how many construction sites are eliminated. In doing so, you might want to revisit point #20. In the future, take care only of those things that you can really influence and that are your responsibility.

35. If you feel the need to get involved and help, then don't waste your time on the dramas of individuals who should confidently solve them themselves. Instead, look for something you are passionate about, something you care about, something you find beautiful and worth protecting, and look around for suitable voluntary work in cooperation with like-minded people. It is good and important to commit yourself to something and to care about something that is bigger than yourself and points beyond you.

36. But what do you do when people you care about have a problem that is overwhelming to them and they turn to you? Be there, show understanding, and accept what is there. Comfort them when necessary. Then look for a solution together, consider whether you can support (not step in) or whether professional support needs to be sought. E.g. in case of addiction problems, you are also nobody's therapist and certainly not mental garbage can, where the other person unloads, refuels new energy, and returns to an ongoing situation unchanged, e.g. toxic relationship /addiction/ financial problems, etc. You can assist someone emotionally, but here you need to pay special attention to healthy boundaries. It should also be reciprocal, because there comes a time when you want to cry it out and feel understood and accepted. That's all it should be about. If you revolve around the same issue several times, there is pathology in it - so be careful. Again, the problems of others should not become yours, even if the people are close to your heart. Here you can support within the framework of common sense, the problems must be addressed by the other person himself, if necessary with professional help. Especially when it comes to psychological or addiction issues, many people shy away from the expert. I like to say: if your tooth hurts, you don't go down to the basement, get the drill and say: "I'll do it myself!

Even if you face your problems with help, there is still enough to do for yourself, it is about saving mistakes and unnecessary setbacks, and to tackle the problem as effectively as possible. The doing is still up to you.

37. How else to avoid problems: in Polish there is a saying that it is a good habit not to lend anything (Dobry zwyczaj, nie pozyczaj). As a rule, you run after your stuff, get things broken or damaged, or don't get them back at all. You definitely don't get any benefit from it, only trouble with it. With money it looks even worse, with small amounts some are not conscientious at all in returning them, with large ones lending can lead to very big problems for you. Nothing shows the true colors of a family like an inheritance... Lent money can too. Beware of becoming someone's second bank and regular source of money when theirs runs out, that is a black hole and absolutely not your responsibility to fill it. Never give money to addicts.

However, from the movie "In the Streets of the Bronx" there is a life hack that definitely works with lent money. There is a scene where the young man, who is a protégé of a mobster, complains that a guy who still owes him $20 has been running away from him ever since. In response, the mobster asks him if he likes the guy and if $20 is a lot to him. Since the boy denies both, the mobster says, "Then be glad to be rid of him for $20." Lend if then well calculated... wink, wink

38. That brings us to the subject of money in general. I'm definitely not an authority on the subject of money, but here (besides lending it) are a few things I've learned from my own wallet: it's not true that money corrupts character. It only enhances it because you can do more. Being too generous financially doesn't pay off. As a rule, others don't give you anything.

39. On money management:

don't go into consumer debt, at most buy a property on credit, this should not exceed 20% of your monthly income. Do not live beyond your means, spend less than you earn and create a financial cushion so that life can rarely put your with your back against the wall. Everything else is optional and whether and how you invest your money is then up to you. But if you follow the above rules, your money will not be able to make you unhappy, which is very important. With a plus in your account you will also sleep better. The thing that is so great about financial freedom (to whom it is granted) is not the stuff you can buy, but the feeling of never having to do anything about money again and being the master of your time. At least that's what I've heard.

40. Money or not, the most precious commodity is peace of mind. We get it robbed by others and circumstances it seems, but most of all it is robbed by our own head (see my book: "Radical Practice Peace of Mind") .Aptly described by Sandra Parker in her book: "Embracing Unrest"[20] : "Worry brings with it a (false) sense of control. Worriers are sure they should worry even if the odds of their anxious prediction are so small that they would be the winner of a lottery with the signs reversed if their prediction came true. When you worry, you lose yourself in a story. You don't realize you are worrying to avoid unrest. You are sure that something "out there" needs your attention. Worry distracts *you from the vulnerable truth that you have no ultimate control or certainty*.

Worry is not the same as healthy planning. It is a playing out of scary possibilities, imagining that the "what ifs" will prevent or manage them.

The terrible irony is that you live in an imaginary world where bad things keep happening, if you avoid turmoil and believe that you can't bear what it would feel like if bad things happened." [21]

With rumination and negative thought spirals, you screw up your own life. If you want to ruminate on scenarios, or "anticipate" them, in order to protect yourself, so please see that this is a misguided and not effective, but a very self-harming "self-protective measure" from childhood. It once served to give you the illusion of control where you were helpless as a matter of fact, and to ease the pain you felt by deluding yourself into thinking "solutions" and distracting yourself from the unbearable feelings by circling your thoughts. Well learned, this still works today, in case the emotional situation is similarly bad, and this coping tool is the only one available and additionally well practiced. What is to be done instead? Ask yourself:

"What is actually happening at this moment? Only danger justifies a protective fight or flight action. Is it a danger (threat to life and limb at the moment)? If so, fight or flee. Is it about vulnerability (rising emotions, uncertainty, limits of control - in other words, agitation)? If so, calm the body through turned interest and non-judgment. Is it fear (threatening movies and stories about the future or past)? If so, block the scary story and calm the body. Note: "Future danger" is not danger; it is fear because it is not present in the moment. Does paying attention to the sensations reduce the arousal or keep it elevated? If the arousal does not subside, look for a movie or story playing in the background that is preventing you from being present. The biggest indicator that a scary movie is on is unrelenting physical arousal despite your patient, heartfelt interest and non-judgment. Are you telling what you feel, or are you in the moment and feeling your body? What is actually happening in this moment?

WHAT TO DO: Remember that anxiety is the escape from restlessness created by stories. Simply paying attention to body sensations while the stories continue will not ease your distress. You need to distinguish between anxiety and restlessness. Restlessness is soothed by paying attention; anxiety keeps returning. Name the story and see how it tries to lead you away from vulnerable reality. Decide to stop giving energy to this story. Then feel the anxiety until it melts in the warmth of your inner attention.[22]

When you become fully aware that the circling of thoughts and worrying is just a pointless, supposed protective mechanism that only harms you, robs you of all energy and poisons yor life, it will be easier for you to let go of it. Say STOP to thoughts and ground yourself in the present, feel into your body, feel your emotions. Feel what it is all about:

41. When you feel tension, it actually only indicates an opportunity for growth. The better you are in contact with all your emotions, the better you can read them and also endure them without wanting to "make them go away" directly, the more you can learn about yourself and the more mature you are as a person. The more peace of mind you will have. To have it, as I understand it now, does not mean to be in eternal (subdued) equanimity, or to be eternally exuberantly blissful, but it is about: "So for every living being it is not about reaching a state, but about shaping a process. Therefore, what Aaron Antonovsky called a "sense of coherence" should more aptly be called a "sense of coherence-restoration-competence." However, this conviction that there is nothing left in the world that is capable of threatening one's inner equilibrium, and to be able to find a suitable solution to all disturbances and problems, can only be formed by a person who has had the experience throughout his or her life that he or she has been able to solve and master various problems and challenges that arise in life in such a way that the

accompanying incoherence in one's own brain could always be transformed into a somewhat more coherent state. People who have this feeling are to be envied. They are happy, they stay healthier, they shape their lives with joy and ease, and they don't stop rejoicing throughout their lives at every further development of their own."[23] However, I would like to encourage you, because the quote suggests that only a select few lucky people manage to do this, to take things on. Even if you have not lived in the state of coherence as much as possible so far due to your childhood and other conditioning by your previous life experiences (how to achieve coherence and establish it in your life, and how to deal with your emotions, I describe in detail in my previous books), you are now an adult and can start doing so from now on. The thing to understand here and now is that the only thing you have to do is just to die. Everything else is optional, but everything you do or don't do inevitably brings consequences for you. Our most immature and self-inhibiting (non) choices as adults are the ones we make to avoid feeling difficult emotions or out of fear (usually of social consequences, and the prospect of then being alone). In the end it is we ourselves who prevent us from facing life and other people at eye level, and from looking for solutions that are appropriate to us.

42. And so the circle closes: all our problems result from not wanting to see our emotions, not wanting to feel them, being afraid of the consequences of what we actually want, being afraid of being excluded by others. (See point 1). De Mello was right when he said, "The path of the enlightened man is lonely." This does not mean that you cannot be among people. However, you are then free. To some of them, however, you are a threat because the usual "buttons" don't work for you. Are you seriously afraid of "losing" such idiots? Wake up!

43. "Anxiety is an indeterminate feeling of trepidation or concern, originating from influences of little specifiability that are perceived as potentially threatening. Fear, on the other hand, is triggered by concrete stimuli, objects or situations, and results in a fear or alarm response."[24] In points 40 and 41, I addressed it that circling thoughts of possible negative consequences or reliving unpleasant past over and over again is a misguided coping mechanism that keeps itself alive and is fueled if the thoughts are not silenced. This leaves you in a chronic state of alarm (in the sympathetic nervous system) and unable to relax. If you want to know if it is still meaningful planning of possible events, or if it is worrying, the distinction is simple: look at how you feel afterwards, and if there is an afterwards at all. Planning is, for example, making a business plan, thinking about structures and processes and how you might optimize them; considering what issues you want to address in a conversation, professional or personal, and what outcome you're aiming for (with the clarity that it doesn't necessarily have to turn out that way). At some point, you'll be satisfied with the ideas and will be done with the topic. Thought circles do not take a natural end and you suffer more and more. The recommendations from the points above will help you stop this pointless suffering. The absence of suffering can already contribute a lot to our happiness; it is a necessary condition especially in pathological unnecessary self-inflicted pain. I would like to thoroughly talk you out of worrying, as you see, because the price is enormous.

44.   What you need instead is the basic attitude, *"Whatever life brings me, I can face it and find ways to deal with it in my best (long-term) interest."* You don't have to like what happens or have it go your way; life inevitably brings problems and challenges. But you trust yourself to get over it, and rely on yourself. Many of the diffuse fears that we grind in mind mills and still can't get down are not really rooted in

the fact that we don't know (and can't know) what someone else might do to us, but that we don't trust ourselves to stand up for ourselves when it is necessary. That is the crucial point.

45. If you can live this attitude, you will be able to face things in a more relaxed and serene way. Stress will inevitably come and shoot you out of the parasympathetic nervous system into the sympathetic nervous system. However, with all the resources you have, you can actively take care of your well-being. Since we are not only thinking heads but also feeling bodies, it is important to reduce the stress response in the body. A large part of our chronic stress is due in part to the fact that we no longer fully go through the body's natural stress response. For one thing, the triggers are usually no longer in the "danger to life and limb" category, and fight or flight is not appropriate as a response to social stress, for example, and is suppressed. And this is where the real problem begins. A reaction that is beneficial and health-promoting in itself, is inhibited and thereby becomes a problem itself. "Your body loves acute stress. This process of climax and recovery - the action of the sympathetic nervous system followed by the action of the parasympathetic nervous system that triggers cellular cleansing and repair - is wonderful for us. In fact, we need it. Just as your house needs regular cleaning, so do your cells, and acute stress is a process by which this cleaning occurs. We need rest and relaxation, yes, but we also need positive stress. We need both. Especially as we age, we tend to have lower vagal tone at rest, which leads to sluggish autonomic stress responses: We get less of the sharp on-off responses in the branches of the nervous system. This makes it all the more important to get "positive stress." When we intentionally and repeatedly inflict acute stress on ourselves, we harness our natural ability to get stronger. We know this is beneficial - that it's healthy for the body and that it helps us deal with future stress. In animal studies with organisms like mice and worms, short bursts of hormetic stress have actually been

shown to prolong life."[25] That means you need to physically relieve pent-up stress in your daily life without punching anyone in the face. Sports that get your heart rate up are great for this. Work with a punching bag, do interval runs or HIIT. After that, you can deepen the recovery that is only then possible. If, after a stressful day, trying to meditate away the tension has left you feeling angry, here's the explanation: you need to metabolize the stress before you can relax. Then you can also reap the full benefits of meditation. (More about this in Radical Practice Peace of Mind, so I won't repeat it here).

46. Repetition, however, is the key to everything: "You will never change your life until you change your daily habits. The secret to your success is in your daily routine." Darren Hardy

You repeat something all day long, whether you are aware of it or not, whether it is beneficial for you or not. Even our thoughts are more than 90 percent the same as those of the previous day, which explains why we are swimming in the same sauce forever, and swimming away from it is so incredibly difficult. Now it's time again for a de Mello quote, "Awareness, awareness and awareness." You really need that. You need to be aware of what it's thinking to you all day, and when you catch yourself in thought spirals, interrupt them immediately, and exchange them for beneficial and helpful thoughts, such as: "No matter what, I can face this."
Since only habit helps against habit: analyze your daily routine and replace bad habits with good ones. (More about this topics in the previous books, especially in "Peace of Mind.") Whereby you hopefully found some ideas for change here, especially concerning your mindset. For your future to flourish, pay attention to point 20 and shape your habits and environment accordingly. And then there is only one thing left to do: do what you have identified as the right thing to do. Over and over again. Until you can't do anything else.

47. Being happy, or whatever you want to call it, is not just the absence of unnecessary suffering. Whereby this already makes a lot of difference. Your attitude is of enormous importance. Here is a short summary according to Dr. Epel: "The unexpected will happen, and that is okay. I can temper my expectations. I can sit back, relax, and let the experience come to me. I can let go of the things I have no control over. I can put down the extra baggage. Stress can be exciting! I can feel motivated and energized by challenges. I can relax and relieve acute stress. My body loves a good stress response. I can let nature do the work of bringing my nervous system back into balance. I am a part of nature. I deserve rest. I will no longer deprive myself of relaxation, sleep and deep rest. Joy shrinks stress. The more I fill my cup with joy, the less I can taste the bitterness of stress and struggle."[26]

48. How best to fill the cup with joy? With gratitude: "It not only feels good, but also contributes to greater well-being and better relationships. Those who are grateful, studies show it clearly, suffer less from anxiety, anger, stress, sleep disturbances, physical symptoms of illness, and depression. Why does gratitude have so many positive effects? One reason, psychologists hypothesize, is that a pleasant emotion like gratitude cannot be felt at the same time as negative emotions like anxiety or anger. Another reason may be that gratitude supports social interaction. After all, gratitude also means connectedness - and that is something that is vital for us. Studies show: Thanking someone else is not only good for you, but also for the person you are thanking. That's because our thanks mean social recognition - an extremely effective way to strengthen relationships. Thanks even have an effect on the person giving thanks. Because those who give thanks subsequently feel more connected to the person they have thanked. Living together becomes more pleasant. And the

effect is multiplied: Those who are together with grateful people also develop more gratitude.

Being grateful makes you happier [and fortunately you can learn to be grateful]. For example, with a gratitude diary, in which you write every day a few experiences for which you can be grateful that day. It doesn't have to be anything big. Many things that we take for granted can be an occasion for gratitude. A beautiful moment when the sun shone through the leaves. A kind gesture from a colleague. The successful meeting with a friend. The fresh air. The fact that it's not raining today. Or that it is finally raining again after a long drought. That you are healthy or not in pain at the moment. Or that there is food on the table on a regular basis.[27] Gratitude beats many things by far.

49. Otherwise, go out into nature. Walk slowly. Observe. Feel, hear, taste and smell. Enjoy being part of it.

50. AMOR FATI[28] : You go through life more relaxed if you accept it with all facets, the good, the bad, and do not fight with reality. In the end it is like this: we want to experience something and not be as indifferent like a stone. We want to be touched by life, to be moved, to have something new happen, something unexpected, something that brings spice into everyday life. Most of my most beautiful experiences were absolutely spontaneous, arising from a mood or situation that I knew nothing about in advance. Many successful and special experiences in retrospect grew out of the fact that something went completely wrong. And then something better came along, or completely different things suddenly became possible. You spontaneously came into contact with complete strangers on a deeper level, and it touched you (in this case, me). If you have the confidence that you can hold everything because you have a secure basis in yourself, what should happen?

BIBLIOGRAPHY

1 https://de.wikipedia.org/wiki/Weisheit accessed 11.11.2021

2 https://www.klinikum-nuernberg.de/DE/ueber_uns/Fachabteilungen_KN/kliniken/psychosomatik/leistungen/docs-pics/Corona_Entspannungs_Podcast/Folge_5_Der-Ring.pdf accessed 11/16/2021

3 http://www.allreadable.com/fad3An72 accessed 03/17/2022

4 https://www.freizeit-stuebchen.de/t12096f6-Wie-sind-die-Menschen-hier-in-der-Stadt.html accessed 20.03.2022

5 https://www.jetztnichtmorgen.com/?p=6664 accessed 09/26/2022

6 Roth, Gerhard: Warum es so schwierig ist, sich und andere zu ändern. Klett-Cotta 2020. p. 426 et seq.

7 Ibid. S. 302

8 https://www.bernds-journal.de/lotterie-ein-jiddischer-witz/ accessed 29/09/2022

9 https://www.kirche-im-swr.de/beitraege/?id=15448 accessed 29/09/2022

10 https://utekowalski.de/pages/topics/mist-973.php accessed 29/09/2022

11 Christan Andersen: The Emperor's New Clothes. https://www.labbe.de/Des-Kaisers-neue-Kleider accessed 23.11.2022

12 In this regard, there is a beautiful poem "Friends" by the Polish national poet Adam Mickiewicz:

Przyjaciele

Nie masz teraz prawdziwej przyjaźni na świecie;
Ostatni znam jej przykład w oszmiańskim powiecie.
Tam żył Mieszek, kum Leszka, i kum Mieszka Leszek.
Z tych, co to: gdzie ty, tam ja, - co moje, to twoje.
Mówiono o nich. że gdy znaleźli orzeszek,
Ziarnko dzielili na dwoje;
Słowem, tacy przyjaciele,
Jakich i wtenczas liczono niewiele.
Rzekłbyś; dwójduch w jednym ciele.

O tej swojej przyjazni raz w cieniu dąbrowy
Kiedy gadali, łącząc swojo czułe mowy
Do kukań zozul i krakań gawronich,
Alić ryknęło raptem coś koło nich.
Leszek na dąb; nuż po pniu skakać jak dzięciołek.
Mieszek tej sztuki nie umie,
Tylko wyciąga z dołu ręce: "Kumie!"
Kum już wylazł na wierzchołek.

Ledwie Mieszkowi był czas zmrużyć oczy,
Zbladnąć, paść na twarz: a już niedźwiedź kroczy.
Trafia na ciało, maca: jak trup leży;
Wącha: a z tego zapachu,
Który mógł być skutkiem strachu.
Wnosi, że to nieboszczyk i że już nieświeży.
Więc mruknąwszy ze wzgardą odwraca się w knieję,
Bo niedźwiedź Litwin miąs nieświeżych nie je.

Dopieroż Mieszek odżył... "Było z tobą krucho! -
Woła kum, - szczęście, Mieszku, że cię nie zadrapał!
Ale co on tak długo tam nad tobą sapał.
Jak gdyby coś miał powiadać na ucho?"
"Powiedział mi - rzekł Mieszek - przysłowie niedźwiedzie:

Że prawdziwych przyjaciół poznajemy w biedzie".

https://literat.ug.edu.pl/amwiersz/0023.htm accessed on 01.10.2022

[13] https://www.lateinheft.de/phaedrus/phaedrus-fabulae-101-lupus-et-agnus-ubersetzung/ accessed on 01.10.2022

[14] https://www.garten-literatur.de/Leselaube/andersen_entlein.htm accessed 12/26/2022

[15] https://mbsr-achtsamhochdrei.de/die-alte-frau-und-die-gluecksbohnen/ accessed on 01.04.2023

[16] De Mello, Anthony, "Der springende Punkt. Wach werden und glücklich sein." Herder 2011. p. 71

[17] A great book on this is "The body keeps the score" by Bessel van der Kolk.

[18] Pries, Mirriam MD: "Burnout kommt nicht nur von Stress." Südwest. 2020.

[19] Cloud, H; Townsend, J. "Nein sagen ohne Schuldgefühle." SCM Hännssler. 2017. S.169

[20] Parker, Sandra Dr.: Embracing Unrest: Harness Vulnerability to Tame Anxiety and Spark Growth. Page Two Press. 2022.

[21] Ibid. pp. 203, 204 Emphasis mine.

[22] Ibidem p. 208ff

[23] Hüther, Gerald: Lieblosigkeit macht krank. Ullstein 2022. p.98ff

[24] https://www.dasgehirn.info/entdecken/grosse-fragen/angst-beherrscht-man-nicht-ohne-furcht-zu-kennen accessed 16.05.2023

[25] Dr. Epel, Elissa: "The Stress Prescription: Seven Days to More Joy and Ease. Penguin Life. 2022. S. 93

[26] Ibid: p. 203

[27] https://www.tk.de/techniker/magazin/life-balance/wohlbefinden/dankbarkeit-2053330 accessed 16.05.2023

[28] Lat. Love of fate - in the sense of love of the necessary and inevitable (asserted by Nietzsche as a sign of human greatness).